MW00366013

Essential Question
How do we use money?

How to Be a
Smart Shopper

by Jonathan Chen

Money is important. We need it to buy things we need or want. People do not want to **waste** money. That is why it is important to be a smart shopper. Here are some tips.

A smart shopper always has a plan.

Money I have	
Allowance:	$5.00
Saved birthday money:	$15.00
Total:	$20.00
Expenses	
After-school snacks:	$2.00
Movies:	$6.00
Charity:	$2.00
Total:	$10.00

You add up money in a budget.

You need a **budget**. That is a plan for spending or saving money. It tells what things cost. It also tells how much money you have.

Look at Sonja's budget. She has money for snacks and the movies.

Newspaper ads show prices.

Comparison Shopping

Maybe your family wants to buy something. You can **comparison** shop. That means finding out how much the thing you want costs at different places. You can go to stores and check the prices.

You can also use the Internet. The thing you want to buy might cost less if you purchase it on the Internet. A smart shopper gets his or her money's worth.

Shopping on the computer also saves gas money.

STOP AND CHECK

Why is it important to be a smart shopper?

Make a list before shopping. This system will make shopping easier. Planning ahead will give you more value for your money. This way you will not buy things you do not need.

Shopping List

milk

eggs

apples

carrots

lettuce

A shopping list makes your trip to the supermarket faster.

Be sure you have space for things you buy.

Sales and Coupons

Many supermarkets have sales. Look at the ad from the supermarket. Is there something on sale that you use all the time? It is a good idea to buy a lot of those things.

You can find coupons in the newspaper.

Another way to be a smart shopper
is to use coupons. Coupons show an
amount of money you can subtract
from an item's price. Find coupons
for what you need to buy. Give them
to the person who takes your money.
The person who invented coupons
was a smart shopper!

Receipts

Before going home, a smart shopper checks his or her **receipt**. A receipt is a record of what you bought. It also shows how much you paid.

receipt

Always check that the prices are right.

STOP AND CHECK

Why should you make a shopping list?

9

Solving by Sharing

Did you ever want something that costs too much? Maybe you and your sister both want bikes. But there is money for only one bike. You can share.

Sharing things is a good way to save money.

You can invite your neighbors and play together.

You can also share with neighbors. Why not buy one gaming system? Then you can take turns. Make a plan for which days you will play.

Planning Ahead

Sonja and her family want to visit an amusement park. They have a problem. They do not know how much the trip will cost.

When something costs a lot of money, it is a good idea to plan for it. Sonja's family decided to do some **research**. First, they found out how much things will cost. Then they made a graph.

Make a plan before taking a trip.

The graph shows the costs for each person going to the park. Together, lunch and snacks will cost $6.00. The games will cost $8.00. Rides will be $10.00. Sonja's family looked at their budget. Each person had $25.00 to spend on the trip. They had enough money for the trip!

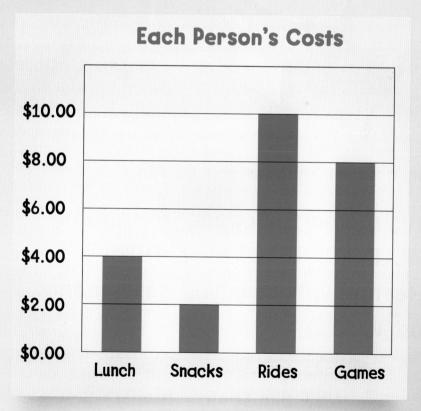

Each Person's Costs

Planning will help you stick to your budget.

Being a smart shopper can be fun.

Being a smart shopper takes some work. But it is worth it. Following these tips will help you save money. Good luck!

STOP AND CHECK

Why did Sonja's family make a graph?

Respond to Reading

Summarize

Use important details to summarize *How to Be a Smart Shopper.*

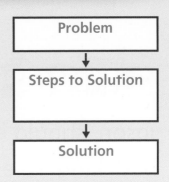

Text Evidence

1. How do you know *How to Be a Smart Shopper* is expository text? Genre

2. How would you solve the problem of not having enough money for an item? Problem and Solution

3. Use paragraph clues to figure out the meaning of *tips* on page 2. Paragraph Clues

4. Write about what comparison shopping is and the problem that it solves. Write About Reading

Compare Texts
Read a myth about chasing after something valuable.

The Golden Fleece

Jason should have been king. But a bad king ruled his land. Jason knew he needed to find the Golden Fleece to get his land back. The Golden Fleece was a special wool. It was hard to find. Jason and some brave men sailed off to find it.

It was a scary trip for Jason and his men. They had to fight monsters. There were also bad storms. It took a long time to find the Golden Fleece, but they found it. Jason and the men brought it home.

Jason gave the king the Golden Fleece. He asked for the throne. The greedy king said no. He chased Jason and his men, but he could not catch them. Jason hid from the king for the rest of his life. He never became a king, but he did have many adventures!

Make Connections
Why do we need money?
Essential Question

What is valuable to different people in each selection? Text to Text

Glossary

budget *(BUHD-jit)* a plan for spending money *(page 3)*

comparison *(kuhm-PAR-uh-suhn)* seeing how things are alike or different *(page 4)*

receipt *(ree-SEET)* a piece of paper that shows what you bought *(page 9)*

research *(REE-surch)* finding out information or facts *(page 12)*

waste *(WAYST)* to spend money without thinking *(page 2)*

Index

Focus on
Social Studies

Purpose To make and read a budget bar graph

What to Do

Step 1 With a partner, make a bar graph for a trip like the one on page 13.

Step 2 Decide which thing costs the most.

Step 3 Decide which thing costs the least.

Step 4 Talk about why you should plan before spending money.